SAVE EARTH'S ANIMALS!

Endangered Animals of ANTARCTICA and the ARCTIC

Marie Allgor

PowerKiDS press™

New York

Published in 2011 by The Rosen Publishing Group, Inc.
29 East 21st Street, New York, NY 10010

First Edition

Editor: Jennifer Way
Book Design: Julio Gil

Photo Credits: Cover Thomas Kokta/Getty Images; pp. 4, 5 (inset), 7, 10, 12–13, 21 (top), 22 Shutterstock.com; p. 5 (top) Harry Gerwin/Getty Images; pp. 6, 8 iStockphoto/Thinkstock; p. 14 Hemera/Thinkstock; p. 9 Jupiterimages/Photos.com/Thinkstock; p. 15 © Lacz, Gerard/Animals Animals-Earth Scenes; pp. 16, 17 Matthias Breiter/Getty Images; p. 18 Maria Stenzel/Getty Images; p. 19 © OSF/Fleetham, D./Animals Animals-Earth Scenes; p. 20 © Morales/age fotostock; p. 21 (inset) Flip Nicklin/Getty Images.

Library of Congress Cataloging-in-Publication Data

Allgor, Marie.
   Endangered animals of Antarctica and the Arctic / By Marie Allgor. — 1st ed.
      p. cm. — (Save earth's animals!)
   Includes index.
   ISBN 978-1-4488-2534-9 (library binding) — ISBN 978-1-4488-2652-0 (pbk.) —
ISBN 978-1-4488-2653-7 (6-pack)
   1. Endangered species—Polar regions—Juvenile literature. 2. Wildlife conservation—Polar regions—Juvenile literature. I. Title.
   QL104.A45 2011
   591.680998—dc22

                                            2010027077

Manufactured in the United States of America

CPSIA Compliance Information: Batch #WW11PK: For Further Information contact Rosen Publishing, New York, New York at 1-800-237-9932

Contents

Antarctica and the Arctic

What do you know about Earth's polar regions? You likely know that they are made up of the lands and waters that surround the North Pole and the South Pole. Antarctica is one of Earth's seven continents. The South Pole is in Antarctica. The Arctic is the region around the North Pole. The Arctic crosses many continents, including North America, Europe, and Asia.

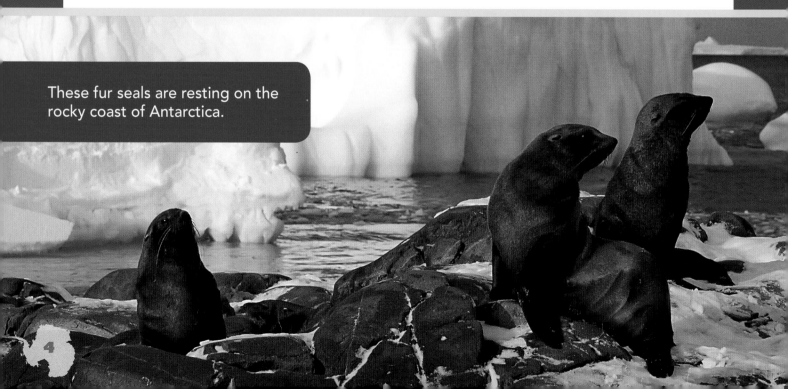

These fur seals are resting on the rocky coast of Antarctica.

This is an oil-drilling rig in the North Atlantic Ocean. Drilling for oil can hurt the environment and animals around the rig.

This is a walrus, which lives in the Arctic.

Both polar regions are cold and icy places. People have changed and hurt Earth's **environment**, and this has changed and hurt the polar regions, too. Many animals that live in these places are endangered.

Polar Climates

The weather a place has over a long time is called its climate. Antarctica and the Arctic have cold, dry weather all year. Antarctica's usual temperatures are around -56° F (-49° C). The Arctic's temperatures are a bit warmer at -29° F (-34° C).

The Arctic is made up of an ocean with land all around it. It receives between 24 and 49 inches (60–125 cm) of **precipitation** each year.

Polar bears live in Arctic regions. Their fat keeps them warm even when they are swimming in icy water.

Adélie penguins, shown here, are one of the kinds of penguins that live in Antarctica.

Antarctica is an island. Most of Antarctica is a desert. The coasts get up to 40 inches (101 cm) of precipitation, though.

Polar Habitats

The polar regions are cold, treeless tundra habitats. Many animals have special **adaptations** that let them live in these habitats. Many polar animals have fat, called blubber, under their skin. They also often have fur or feathers that **insulate** their bodies.

Antarctica has rocky shores, hard-packed sheets of ice, and a warmer but stormy

Birds such as the southern giant petrel live on the islands around Antarctica.

Harp seals live in the Arctic. They have both fur and thick layers of fat to help keep them warm.

peninsula. Penguins, seals, and many birds use these places to have babies or to live year-round.

In the Arctic, polar bears and seals live on the ice all year. Other animals visit the Arctic during the warmer summer months. They find food or mate and then leave before winter.

Endangered Polar Animals

Global climate change is causing ice in the Earth's polar regions to melt. This has an effect on the polar regions' animals. If things do not change, the animals on these pages could one day become extinct.

MAP KEY

- Blue Whale
- Eskimo Curlew
- Hooded Seal
- Northern Royal Albatross
- Peary Caribou
- Polar Bear

Hooded Seal

1. Blue Whale

Blue whales are the largest animals on Earth. They are almost as long as an airplane and weigh as much as 40 elephants!

2. Polar Bear

Polar bears are listed as **vulnerable** to becoming endangered in the next 100 years. There are fewer than 25,000 polar bears living in the wild.

3. Hooded Seal

Hooded seals spend much of their lives in the cold waters of the northern Atlantic. Their numbers have gone down by 30 percent worldwide. Today they are vulnerable to extinction.

4. Peary Caribou

The Peary caribou lives in the High Arctic Islands. There are fewer than 2,000 of these caribou left on Earth.

Antarctica
(South Pole)

Arctic
(North Pole)

UNITED STATES

CANADA

RUSSIA

GREENLAND

5. Northern Royal Albatross

The northern royal albatross is a huge, black-and-white albatross. It lives in the waters around Antarctica. Scientists guess that there are fewer than 17,000 of these birds living in the wild.

6. Eskimo Curlew

The eskimo curlew is listed as critically endangered. Its numbers have become so low that scientists are studying this bird's Arctic and South American habitats to find out if it has become extinct.

Polar Bear

Polar bears are built for life in the Arctic. They have thick fat under their skin that insulates them from the cold. The polar bear's thick, white fur also keeps it warm. It helps the bear blend in with its snowy habitat, too. Polar bears are more in danger of being too hot than too cold!

Polar bears' white fur helps them get close to the animals they eat without being seen!

Many scientists believe global climate change is causing polar ice to melt. This could mean trouble for polar bears. Polar bears need this ice to live. If we cannot find a way to stop climate change, polar bears might go from vulnerable to endangered or extinct.

Northern Royal Albatross

The northern royal albatross is one of Antarctica's many endangered sea bird **species**. It lives in the waters around Antarctica and nests on islands including New Zealand and islands off the tip of South America.

The northern royal albatross's numbers have gone down for many reasons. Some have died due to storms and habitat loss. Nonnative animals, such as cats, also hunt and eat these

Trash floating in oceans not only hurts fish, but also birds such as the northern royal albatross.

Northern royal albatross are large birds. Adults are nearly 4 feet (120 cm) long and weigh about 15 pounds (7 kg).

albatross. Albatross are hurt by pollution, too. There is a lot of plastic floating in the oceans. Albatross often eat it by mistake. They then feel too full to eat food and die from hunger. There are fewer than 8,000 breeding pairs of northern royal albatross left.

Peary Caribou

Peary caribou live only on the Canadian Arctic islands. Peary caribou spend most of the year eating **lichen**. However, in the Arctic winters there is no lichen. They must use their sharp hooves to paw through the ice. Under the ice they find dried grasses and other plants.

Peary caribou numbers began dropping in the 1970s. The numbers are still dropping today. Climate

Peary caribou are a subspecies of reindeer. A subspecies is a very closely related animal within a species.

This is lichen. Lichen is one of the few things that grow in the Arctic.

change has hurt the caribou's habitat. Today there are only around 700 Peary caribou left. Scientists took 25 of them from their habitat to start a **captive breeding** program. It is hoped that this program will save the animal from extinction.

Blue Whale

Blue whales are huge! They are around 100 feet (30 m) long. You would think that such large animals must eat a lot of big fish, right? In fact, these giants eat tons of tiny, shrimplike animals called krill.

Up until the mid-1800s, blue whales were too big for people to hunt. By 1868, someone had found a way to better hunt whales.

Krill, shown here, are found in oceans all over the world. A blue whale can eat up to 40 million krill in a day!

Blue whales do not have teeth. Instead they have comblike baleen plates. Baleen plates let them take in large amounts of water and krill. The baleen plates let most of the water out while keeping the krill inside.

It is thought that 99 percent of blue whales were killed by whalers. Scientists guess that between 8,000 and 14,000 blue whales live in the world's oceans today.

Hooded Seal

Hooded seals live in the seas north of the Arctic Circle. They have their babies on the ice there. The seal gets its name from its nose. Part of the adult male's nose grows larger than the rest. It forms a large bump, or hood, on its forehead. The seal can make the hood blow up in a large bubble from its nose.

The hooded seal has been banned for **commercial** hunting since 1987.

Here is a hooded seal with its hood blown up. Males blow up their hoods when they are trying to draw mates to them.

This is a hooded seal baby, or pup. In male hooded seals, the hood starts to grow when the seal is about four years old.

The hooded seal eats mussels, squid, shrimp, fish, and starfish, shown here. Aside from people, who hunt them for their skin, killer whales are their biggest enemy.

There are many of these seals still in the ocean, but this number is much lower than in the past and the numbers are dropping. For this reason hooded seals are listed as vulnerable animals and may be listed as endangered in the future.

Save the Polar Animals!

Life in Earth's polar regions is not easy. The animals that live in this habitat face danger from global climate change. Changes in the polar climates could cause habitat loss for many animals. This is especially true for animals that live on polar ice that is in danger of melting.

People have passed laws to control hunting and fishing. People have also set aside land that is just for plants and animals to live. However, stopping climate change is not easy. Time will tell if we are doing enough to save our polar animals.

ADAPTATIONS (a-dap-TAY-shunz) Changes in animals that help them live.

CAPTIVE BREEDING (KAP-tiv BREED-ing) Bringing animals together to have babies in a zoo or an aquarium instead of in the wild.

COMMERCIAL (kuh-MER-shul) Having to do with a business or a trade.

ENVIRONMENT (en-VY-ern-ment) All the living things and conditions of a place.

EXTINCT (ek-STINGKT) No longer existing.

GLOBAL CLIMATE CHANGE (GLOH-bul KLY-mut CHAYNG) A slow increase in how hot Earth is. It is caused by gases that are let out when people burn fuels such as gasoline.

INSULATE (IN-suh-layt) To cover something and stop heat or sound from flowing out of it.

LICHEN (LY-ken) Living things that are made of two kinds of living things, called an alga and a fungus.

PRECIPITATION (preh-sih-pih-TAY-shun) Any moisture that falls from the sky. Rain and snow are precipitation.

SPECIES (SPEE-sheez) One kind of living thing. All people are one species.

VULNERABLE (VUL-neh-ruh-bel) In state where someone or something could be easily hurt.

Index

Web Sites

Due to the changing nature of Internet links, PowerKids Press has developed an online list of Web sites related to the subject of this book. This site is updated regularly. Please use this link to access the list: www.powerkidslinks.com/sea/antarc/